DIARY OF A CROSSING GUARD

STARGELL AND MOSLEY

Carolina Ayala-Velasquez

Carolina M-G Ayala-Velasquez

Alameda, CA

Carolina Ayala-Velasquez

Ordering Information:
Amazon. Or reach out to me through Instagram "crossguardchronicles"

Diary Of A Crossing Guard/ Carolina Ayala-Velasquez. — 1st ed.
ISBN 979-8-9855006-2-2

WHAT IS A DIARY?

A DIARY IS A JOURNAL OF SOME
KIND THAT YOU WRITE YOUR
"DAILY" THOUGHTS AND FEELINGS
IN. WHEN I WAS GROWING UP IT
WAS WHERE YOU WOULD WRITE
YOUR SECRETS THAT YOU DIDN'T
WANT ANYONE ELSE TO KNOW.
IN THIS CASE, I AM OK WITH
LETTING YOU ALL KNOW SOME OF
MY REAL-LIFE EXPERIENCES
WHILE BEING A CROSS GUARD.
MANY OF THESE ENTRIES COME
STRAIGHT FROM MY FB DIARY AND
JOURNALS/NOTES IN MY PHONE.
THESE DO MOSTLY FOCUS
AROUND MY CROSS-GUARD PART
OF MY LIFE.

(WHEN YOU ARE WRITING IN YOUR
OWN "DIARY", GUESS WHAT?
GRAMMAR AND ALL THAT DOESN'T
MATTER. JUST YOUR STORY TO
TELL.)

This book is dedicated to the families and people who crossed my path at stargell and mosley in 2022. Thank you for inspiring me, joining me in community and fun and "purpose." Thank you for giving my days more meaning, that I didn't even know about until our time together.

Thank you to my family. For inspiring me daily to be the best version of myself. You are my reason for all I do and I hope to help create a life you love; or support you in creating it.

I am not speaking for all crossing guards or people in this book. I am just sharing my experiences and journey.

Any names used in this book are made up and not the names of the actual people I met.

1/23 and 1/26
"School crossing guards work a brief shift in the morning and afternoon, we work outdoors and on school days only. You will not work weekends, nights or holidays. This is a part time job. Compensation is $60 a day (when you work both shifts.) for less than 3 hours a day."

I will admit, the job description on indeed.com got me. I applied twice, in hopes of getting the job. Or at least a chance at it. I won't lie, for $30 an hour, I thought to myself- I can't pass that up. I thought the hours were great for me since my kids are home doing online school and my other work is from home. My first thoughts were- I could possibly get in some exercise, walking or biking; depending on the location I get and that would benefit me.

2/8/22
"On behalf of All City Management Services Inc, congratulations on completing your initial onboarding paperwork!" Is such a beautiful e-mail to receive. I feel like this is a step in the right direction. Fingerprints are done, intake form done and now I wait for training day.
I had a couple of phone calls before today, that lead to this point. The person in charge was very friendly, upfront and explained how

they really need committed people. I was ready to commit.

2.9.22

I am training in the morning; I say this out loud as I am praying for myself and hope others will hold me in their thoughts as well. I am tomorrow's future cross guard. Knowing that and saying it, fills my heart with excitement and purpose. It makes me feel like I am spreading my wings to fly. Like so many others, I have been working from home during this pandemic time, and now- I am going out into the work in this way. I feel like I am taking steps into the version of me that I am meant to be at this time in my life.

2.10.22

On the way home, this thought came to me: Your world is as big as you let it be.
I realize how much my world has expanded just by taking on this new job.

Whew, my first morning training as a cross guard.
The corner I have can be both very inactive and then extremely active. In a matter of seconds. You have to watch out for so much, in one little space.

The person training me says he feels very confident and happy with me this morning.

Just in 1 hour, so much was to be learned. I am not perfect and I will grow into comfort to a certain extent.

I am thankful I only had to be in a mask for a "short" period of time.

I feel like coming from a teaching background and being a parent helps but; woah.

So much is running through my mind. To remember and know and be.

Such as:

*You use the whistle only for emergencies.

*You never try to direct traffic, you can only stop traffic.

*When you work before or after your time, you are then a volunteer.

*Ask people riding bikes and scooters, to walk them.

*You can only suggest, you can't force.

*You could be the reason someone is excited to go to school.

Today was a big shift for many.

Many families were so excited and relieved to see a cross guard "finally" in their area to help. For some, they were not used to having to stop (cars and people). I could see they were frustrated with being in a rush or having some pause "enforced."

I have to let those feelings of other people's go and focus on the safety of the people including my own. Focus on the good.
It feels so good to bring a smile to children and families again.
It feels so good to be making a difference.
It is a lot.
It is on the whole other side of the island. It was the only position available.
In a car it's a 5–10-minute drive.
To bus or bike will be different stories.
I am thankful for the ride today and getting to know the area and school I am serving.

Today, on my first day- I found out is an unusual early release day. So, although I am just making it home, I will be leaving again soon to probably explore what biking could look and feel like.
So glad I got sleep last night.
My 3-year-old is already trying to play with my gear. The kids are full of questions. I am excited for any income and am enjoying this feeling of living in my purpose.
It's all big adjustments. Mentally, physically, emotionally.

I decided to bike this afternoon. It has been quite the journey already. At one point I realized I lost papers and I had to bike ride and backtrack my steps. I did find them. I dropped my water bottle several times or more and had to keep stopping. I was 40 minutes early but now I know, I can bike ride within 30 minutes or less. I am getting exercise and making money and that feels good.

I am feeling good in my sweat, today I got an hour bike ride in.

I did my second shift, but my first shift alone.

This morning during training, I learned school was out at a different time than I was originally told. I was happy to be flexible and to end both shifts officially by 1 so that I could feel like I have the rest of the day.

This morning I took the car there and back. It was great considering my husband was able to do that before he started work and because it was my first time seeing my site and getting to know where I'll be working.

I underestimated myself. For my ride on the bike this afternoon, I gave myself an hour and a half to get there. Even with stopping, I made it within 40minutes. I had about an hour to sit in the shade. I later moved because I didn't want anyone to think I was supposed to be working but saw me sitting. I didn't want anyone to think I wasn't doing my job.

This afternoon wasn't as busy as this morning.

Families were excited to see me.

"You don't know how much we appreciate you being here"
Two children I asked this morning to walk their bikes when crossing, saw me this afternoon and got off of their bikes without me asking.
So many "hope you have a good day" and "thank you" from children and adults. So much appreciation and thanks from drivers.

It is amazing the life that is out there, when you get out there.
I loved making a difference today.
I loved being around children and families again.
I loved bike riding, sweating, drinking water, listening to music, enjoying views. I loved feeling like my kids are safe when home.
Thankful for my uncle and our oldest daughter.
Thankful for phones.
Thankful for time.
It was a great first day today.

How many songs will it take until I make it home? I ask myself this as I put on some music thanks to my phone. I share this question on Instagram, to document for me and it's a fun thought.

I am sore from sitting on the bike ride. My hands hurt from holding things while riding.

But it's all good. I have the perfect space for shade and sun at the location I serve.

Tomorrow will be filled with more new experiences.

I know we need more money than what I will be getting, but it's a great start and I am excited to hold this space until summer.

Something I like to do at the end of my day is reflect on the day, notice and name my gratitude's and celebrate all of the wins.

Today I am celebrating better sleep last night, than the night before. I am celebrating my first day of training and work as a cross guard. I am celebrating bike riding to and from work. I found happiness in the sweat. To be able to connect with strangers that are already quickly becoming familiar faces is such a blessing. To be able to bring peace and calm and happiness to others is such a beautiful feeling and knowing. Finding peace through the anxiety and courage with the fears. I am celebrating not having soda since last year. A big win for me today is making time to listen to music. I am celebrating time. Time to dream, to close my eyes and rest, to be ok with the parts of me that I am not ok with. I am celebrating setting alarms, setting intentions and taking action from there. I feel tired but filled with so much goodness.

I feel like I am falling short, today in other areas like: practicing yoga, participating in yoga studies, my virtual online work, taking sea moss, working out, and others.

I also know that I am proud. I am proud for all that is and has been. I even made it to take the kids and dog to the park and just chill there. It was pretty empty. We sat. I let the kids just be. My youngest son was able to make time for his volunteer work. and then I even got my 3-year-old to nap!

Those are some major wins, even if some other things didn't happen.

One day it'll all flow.

For now, it's flowing how it should.

****what wins are you celebrating/acknowledging today?

******What parts of you have you not lived out yet, that you want to?
What's stopping you?

2.11.22
What did your yesterday teach you? That shaped your today?

The hardest part about this morning so far is being sore from yesterday. It feels so good to be up and out by 7am. Thank you work, thank you working legs, thank you music, thank you bike, thank you fresh air, thank you warm clothes, thank you light out, thank you gratitude.

This job, although only my second day- has given me so much of a life I have been missing and wanting. Exercise, biking- consistency. The will to go even when sore and tired. The time outside, because I love it. The fresh air, the sun, the views. Time with music. Movement, sweat, fun, joy, smiles, accomplishment. Time in vision and prayer and gratitude. Time making a difference, building community and supporting children and families.

Cross guard chronicles

Today I gave myself about 35minutes to get to work (knowing I could get there in 30minutes.) Well, pain when sitting on my bike was tough. But, I had to power through, to make it on time. I made it 3 minutes early. I decided I will give myself more time next time, so I can have a moment to breathe before jumping in.

Today one little boy said "Do you remember, you are my friend from yesterday?"

So many appreciative children, parents, families and people crossing.

"You have no idea how much we all appreciate you; this street is so scary to cross."

So many people passing in cars wave, so many tilt their hats and say thanks.

Children, adults, people without kids.

Mostly calm, mostly thankful, mostly happy people.

Yes, I got the one child who is on a bike who does not wait for me and rushes through. But, I have the many on bikes who take time to get off and walk their bikes across, say thank you and more.

I get the occasional older children who refuse to wait for me and go around me.

I remind myself; I can only suggest waiting for me. I can only suggest and share about safety.

So many children walk alone or ahead or behind.

So many rushing, walking and driving.

So many walks of life and I wonder about each person.

It was a great day. My first day of 4 bike rides total, to and from. A nice 2 hours of that. My legs felt it on those last two rides.

I feel so thankful and grateful for all of the people, lessons, curiosity, wonder, sights, smiles, sweat, exercise and time.

2.12.22

I knew it was the weekend and yet I still questioned it when I woke up. Feeling like I was supposed to be at work.

When I came across this cross guard job weeks ago that said $60 a day for less than 3 hours a day. I was like "win!"

I did the math. I calculated what $60 a day could look and feel like. Realistically what could it cover.

I decided it was worth it.

I knew I could get exercise, getting to and from work. I knew I could be flexible to make that morning and afternoon shift happen. I knew this would be in alignment with my love for children and families. I knew it would be a challenge to learn something new, to have to be in a mask and get back out into the world after years of living in my own world I had created thanks to the pandemic.

The pieces moved together quickly. I got the job. I officially started. and I am loving it so much already.

I know I am kind of repeating myself. I guess that happens when you are happy and reflective and take time to acknowledge your thoughts and feelings. We all know money matters. The way we allow it to serve us, will be different from person to person. I realized finding this number, has connected so many things for me- in a way I hadn't thought about before or in a way that is now a reminder.

When you find a number that feels good, you can then think of it in so many other forms. Such as: I can sell two of my new books and make that money. I can lead 1 or 2 or 3 coaching sessions and generate that money

(depending on the charge of each session.) I can do so many things to make sixty dollars.
We can get by, we can be comfortable, we can dream bigger, we can thrive.
It just has to start somewhere. For me, it starts here. It starts now.

2.14.22
On my morning bike ride I noticed hearts created from chalk along a pathway.

So beautiful. I am thankful I am not as sore as Friday. I am thankful for music, fresh air, for warm gloves, for exercise, for pathways, for views and for work
Today's experience on the job has more new situations.
I got a ride to and from in the morning. When I got out of the car, and arrived at work- I did not expect it to be so cold. I jogged in place, kept my mask on- trying to get warm. I rubbed my hands together and tried to put them in my pockets.
One little boy asks me if I know who made the grass. I say no. He gets closer to whisper to me "Elsa made the grass" and as he walks away, he says "It's really true" and I tell him I believe him and thank him for telling me.

What if you had someone who believed you?
Who believed in you?
He didn't need me to believe.

'Cause he already did.

What does it mean to be heard?

The bike ride to and from in the afternoon was different. My legs are feeling it. My Hat flew off once and I had to stop to chase it down. This whole ride was me against the wind but at least I warmed up and brought my gloves this time.
Several fast cars today. A police officer came and sat for a while. Then he pulled up to ask if this area has heavy foot traffic, he was trying to catch someone. Eventually he saw the car he was going for. I felt both safer and worried with him so close by.
The wind was so heavy, it was hard to hold my stop sign with one hand.
Part of my bike ride I decided I wanted to see what it would feel like to ride without music. I found myself singing to myself. More focus on growing pains. More comfort in my hands. Everything is about learning.

It is Valentines Day today. So, Although I have work- I am reflecting on the day and love.
Love is...
Him driving you to work and picking you up within the hour.
Him taking your craziness by letting you warm up your freezing hands on his warm cheeks

and then turning the heater on for you to continue defrosting.

It's having food ready for him to eat once he gets home for his lunch break, even though you had to leave to work.

It's expensive roses for his wife and two daughters and mother-in-law.

It's taking the kids to help pick out gifts to surprise you.

It's getting off work early, to set up the table for when you walk in after biking from your afternoon shift.

It's "thank you" for being the new cross guard.

It's whispers in your ear from a child who tells you Elsa made the grass.

It's watching "rise of the guardians" with your children, while homework can wait.

It's not going to the park because staying warmer inside feels better.

It's making trades with other small business to make dreams come true for both of us.

It's coupons that get us free drinks and food.

It's cooking at home.

It's snuggling on the couch to watch tv shows like catfish and love and hip hop.

Love today is - cancelling appointments, to be present with family.

It's not overworking or overbooking or rushing to make things happen because "here" is where we'd rather be.

It's lots of desserts and chocolates. Before, during and after dinner.

Love is...messages from others about what your book and writing means to them.

It's messages and "happy valentine's day"

Its music of your choice.

It's the time with and without makeup.

Its putting on a pink hoodie you haven't worn in years.

It's warm gloves, for that second shift after you realized how much you needed them that first shift.

It's car rides with your mom to get cream soda, and yet not drinking it because you haven't had soda since last year. So, you chose water instead.

It's dressing up in a dress, just to be inside.

It's paying bills and taking pictures and resting.

This morning I thought the perfect day would be... (hiking, biking, be by the water, hot tub, travel)

I love.... (My family, my friends, life)

Love to me... (is shown and shared and said and felt)

Right now, I would love... (to live in the moments, to be grateful, to worry less)

What would it look like to live a life you love?

2.15.22

By the end of my shift in the morning, the sun finally made it to my side. Thankful.

Hello Tuesday. Life of a cross guard.
This morning my husband drove me to work and picked me up. This time, unlike yesterday I brought my beanie and gloves. It was cold! My hands were still numb and frozen after work, even though I had gloves on. It was hard to keep my work hat over my beanie. I was still cold, even though today was warmer and I wore a bigger sweater than yesterday.
I watched as the sun was making its way out. I enjoyed crossing people and feeling the warmth of the sun even for a moment.
The cars on this street are crazy! You never know if they will stop or not. You get your many who do but those few who just lack patience or what not, those ones are so scary.
My husband hopefully enjoyed time at Starbucks and grabbing dishwasher soap. Not rushing back and forth to get me because he parked the car and took a walk. Not having to be home with the kids because my mom was there. Having some alone time. He said it was weird.
So many thank yous as I crossed people of all ages. I have learned the familiar faces. There is one particular car that drives by with a car full of children and they love to smile and wave.

I am thankful that although today was cold. It was warmer than yesterday and it wasn't windy, so-holding the sign was more manageable.

Driving to work is about 10-20 minutes, depending. The bike ride is 30. Not much difference. But biking means you save gas and money. Biking means exercise, for me it is what I have been telling myself I want to participate in. Biking for me means I feel warmer once I get off the bike, from a 30minute ride. I feel like this exercise will mean I will get to sleep better at night. I love learning it all. I might even try walking one day.

I am thankful for the time, the learning and the community. I daydream of the lives people live. I watch them play in their gated community. I wonder. I see who's rushing and who's taking their time. I see who is relieved because I am there and I see those who feel they don't need me and maybe I am just an extra obstacle for them. Or, maybe it's all in my mind and these thoughts are just assumptions that aren't real.

I love this job. I miss teaching so much. I miss life without masks and the extra pandemic fears.

This afternoon my mom drove me. Although I was ready to bike and "work off" the full feeling I had from eating. My mom wanted to see where I worked. So, that is why I took the ride. She waited in the car until I was done. Enjoying the warmth of her car and games on her phone. It was a breezy yet warmer afternoon than the days before. I was so thankful for the sun.

I definitely prefer warm over cold weather.

When you get home and get straight to laundry, dishes, kids...

Woah... take the uniform off first. Take time to transition.

Tuesday is in full effect. Time to transform. Time to take the chances and take my time.

Today I was up by 6:30. I got to work and my youngest son called me saying he threw up. I had no time to process. So many thoughts rushed through my mind. How much did he throw up? Why did he throw up? What is he feeling? Is he sick? Should I go home? What do I do?

However, I was at work and I had heard enough. I knew enough to believe...valentine's foods yesterday probably got to him. I assigned him to his room until I get home.

When I got home, it wasn't really throw up. Not to minimize his experience, but he feels better now that whatever is out.

I made it to counseling to update her and go over my counseling goals.

Today my mom got us both chipotle and we both shared with the kids. We all put money together to get my husband five guys surprise and drop it off to him at work, something different and unexpected.

I love celebrating people the day after a holiday, especially valentines. To remind them that it's an everyday feeling and appreciation.

Today I got rides to and from work. That 10-minute ride is different than that 30 minute bike ride but all of my options are good.

I have been using the diffusers a lot lately.

I had a little soda today, first time since last year. It wasn't anything special like I thought it would be.

***have you ever given up something and welcomed it back in, only to realize what for?

2.16.22
Just because the sun is out
Doesn't mean it won't be cold.

That is what I learned and realized today. What a Wednesday. Today I was up by 5:50. I woke up in so much more pain than yesterday. Lower back pain, top right shoulder/neck. The back of my head even.

I did 10minutes of yoga this morning to try to stretch through and help myself.

I had water for breakfast. I am so thankful for my mom and husband for the rides to work.

I have been thinking of it for awhile now and today I finally did it.

I am so thankful this morning I remembered and took action. Brought some chalk with me and started writing; "don't forget to smile." I left pictures, gratitude's, questions I have heard the kids ask and hop scotch for them this morning.
Some years ago, someone did chalk art near where I live. I have loved coming across chalk art, so- why not.
I am in a mask when people are crossing. I have to maintain whatever distance. This was another way to connect.

This morning I watched parents and children play hop scotch. I listened as children asked "what does this say"
"Look, so much chalk!"

Teaching is always available.
"Thank you for all of the writings"
My husband even parked around the corner and took a walk to enjoy the streets that I work on, it was so nice to see his face and hear his voice.
All of these families that cross, I now am familiar with so many faces and ways they

come and go. I love that it's only been a short amount of time but yet I feel I have made connections with many.

Yesterday a little girl asked me my name. Today she said "you are Lena right?" and I said yes and then she said "my name is Kylie" These moments are so priceless.

Today's chalk art was so much fun.
It sparked conversations among families.
It engaged families
It created wonder
It helped bring joy, smiles and laughs.
It invited in play from children and adults.
It brought excitement to reading
-definitely filled my cup.

I am so thankful I took the time, that I remembered the chalk. I am already going to miss everyone and also enjoy the next 6 days off.

I went back for my afternoon shift, left earlier on my bike ride to give myself time to reflect on life when I arrived for my shift. I sat in the grass to write about something that came to me.

Then I got out my last piece of chalk and wrote 1 question on the two blocks before making it to my stop.

Followed by "enjoy your time "off" on that last empty block before "mine"

When my last shift was over, I rode my bike to leave. A few blocks in, an adult and child were walking by and he says to the young girl "aw man we missed her" as in they didn't make it to cross with me before I had to leave. They thanked me for being their cross guard and for the chalk work today.

I am overfilled with gratitude, goodness, possibilities and happiness

This morning was extra fun and its my last day before school is out tomorrow/next week.

***What matters?

Today I learned…that comfort matters, more air in my bike tires matter, having a bike with a kickstand and basket and water holder matters. Exercise, vitamin d, sun, warmth and fresh air all matter. Giving myself extra time than just what's needed to "get there/arrive"-matters.

2.17.22

I spent so long asking for sun…and when it came my way, I ended up hiding in the shade.

Does time off excite you or upset you?

(time off of work, kids out of school..)

I am excited for the next 6 workdays off (10 days including weekends) because I get to get back to some rest, time with family, outside, yoga studies and more.

I am not excited when I think about the money I won't be making because of the days off.

As a teacher, I used to get paid on days off. As a cross guard, it's not that way (makes sense) but not great for the money I know I need to bring in this month.

I am focusing on the positives and not so much what can't be/won't be/isn't.

I know that not every parent is excited for when their kids don't have school. No school means different things for everyone.

whatever it means for you.

Please make time for what your soul care needs.

Have you ever felt grateful but unhappy?

At the same time.

Can you be both?

I know that both have been true for me at times in life.

So many people have come to me to help them find gratitude and positivity.

I will admit, I am good at this. I kind of always have been.

Sometimes I think "Why do I have to be so positive, just let me be angry/sad...insert feeling"

Sometimes I think "I am grateful but that doesn't mean I am happy"- does that make me ungrateful? Gratitude brings happiness, so why am I not fully happy all the times.

Sometimes I am so grateful for gratitude and I don't always understand myself.

While home, between shifts I joined the virtual milestone hike with Julie from mothersquest. It was emotional. I felt the nerves of hoping the person I invited would feel like this experience is good for them. I left feeling like I am feeling done with goals. I just want to be present. I am very much a "to do list" "goals list" lists, lists, lists - person. Calendars, planners, vision board.... today I just want to be done. These past couple of years I have marked so much off the bucket lists, dream lists, goals lists, to do lists- I am living dreams. I have accomplished so much. and I always have more on my lists. but I am feeling at a bit of a standstill.

I need to be present with all that has been done, is going and can be.

I need to dream again. I need to figure some things out. things I am not even sure of.

What I did feel sure of in that last moment, was not "caring" about the lists. Not even fully feeling all the goodness that's been. Some fear/sadness of comparing then to now and what the future should or could be.

When I vision 2022 all I see is laughter, comfort, happiness and peace. That's the dream. Nothing specific like learning to drive or making a book.

I just want to feel home. to feel safe, stable and like it won't be taken.
I just want to be present, home and enjoying the life we have learned to create and live.

I started this new job as a cross guard last week. Today is only day 6.
Tomorrow there is no school and next week as well. So, I have no work.
I have enjoyed every day of new learnings, experiences, and situations.
yesterday I heard so many times "thank you so much, you have no idea how much we appreciate you. These streets are so crazy, we are so thankful you are here"
Yesterday someone stopped to ask "do you know what happened to the older gentleman who used to be the cross guard?" I don't. I heard there hasn't been a cross guard in this area in a long while. I hope one day when I am not working here anymore, that I leave a mark like him.

2/18/22
I worked my first 6 days as a cross guard and payday is 7 days away. I am so excited to make bill money. I am so excited for the time I have been having.

2.20.22
Making a "splash", making it "big", getting "heard", getting "recognition" for

something…may be one of the goals or driving force and may even happen.

But the true goal and real drive, is the peace that comes with telling your story.

Getting it done, because it matters to you.

Because you need healing and closure and peace.

Anything extra is a bonus.

2.21.22

When you don't have work today and no holiday pay. But you sold a couple of books and made more than your days' pay. Great way to begin. I am grateful.

Hello Monday. I am enjoying knowing the kids have no school today.

We spent some time at the park.

2.23.22

I don't not feel like a master of grief.

I do not feel like I have closure or will ever.

The book I created (Healing While Hurting, poetry and reflections) was a big part of a peace I had never been able to reach before. It does not mean I don't still grieve or I am fully healed. But it was definitely created from my pain and medicine for my healing journey.

I feel like right now, in this moment-in my life, the losses I am feeling are the losses of old stories. Old parts of me that I have outgrown or grown into. People and spaces that I have grown away from. Relationships due to the pandemic that have shifted or gone but I don't necessarily feel grief- because I embraced the good. The good of going inward and growing me. The good from living dreams. The good from growing from pain and making peace with surrender and change.

I don't feel like I ignore my grief or feelings. I feel like I feel my feelings well. That I allow myself to. Because I have been embracing the good, does not mean I have been ignoring the grief or hard stuff. I just created new relationships with me, my pain, my growth and my journey.

the pandemic has brought much grief. In many ways and layers.

grief comes with not just death. but loss of relationships, self, jobs, homes, pets, things...ideas....

I am not all healed or fixed or done just because I am not feeling the way I used to.

2.24.22
Making these books real, is what matters right now.

classes I wish I had as a child:
*cooking
foods and what they support
healthy eating
money mindset
*more music
*more counseling options

*business classes, to learn about credit cards and credit scores and credit in general
*to learn about money, housing, loans,
*home ownership
*driving
*what it means to have a bank account. savings
*how to garden
*holistic and herbal medicines
*to learn about animals
*recycling
* how to invest in yourself
*traveling, hiking
real life experiences
*grief support
*learning about ones ancestry
*how to fix a flat tire (bike, car)
*how to resource and be resourceful
*how to write resume
*marketing
*impacts of social media. technology, fresh air, exercise, eating healthy, being mindful
*meditation
*what it means to have insurance, healthcare
*A will
*Life insurance

I am a mother to 4 and I want all of this and more for them. For everyone's children

When I think of and speak of "Ratchet Grandma" the series.

I light up inside and outside.

All of the visions I have, I can feel as if they are real already.

I just know this is going to be big. For itself, for me, our family, my mom.

I can see my mom doing book signings, even a tv show.

I can see children's books, pg. 13 books and rated R (most ratchet).

I can see merchandise. I see people in the clothing and everything.

The next thing on my to do list is to get us an iPad pro and the procreate app so we can learn to be the illustrator of our dreams.

I do not know the perks of having a publisher and what not. But I can't see us not being in charge of our own story and creation.

This whole creation, came because we couldn't see ourselves in the books we had.

so, we created our own.

Not having the illustrator of my dreams has been "holding me back" but this has been years in the making.

and although I have created books in the meantime. This one stays on my heart.

I want my mom here, alive to enjoy it all.

I have to make this happen.

It's too exciting not to.

The fact that so many people keep asking me when can they buy one and when will it be ready....

I am so ready to make it real.

Like, really real.
my dream vision real.

2.25.22
today was my first pay day. 6 days of work. I actually got paid more than expected.
I am concerned if the "right" amount of taxes were taken out. I feel like it wasn't much and don't want it to affect our future tax experiences.
No clue how to know and do better or how to make changes.
Excited to pay bills. So happy that Credit cards are paid off.

2.26.22
It is amazing how a small change and shift can create so much happiness and opportunity.

2.27.22
When I think back on life. Do I have some thoughts now of what I wish I "should have" or "could have" done? Yes, I have a few thoughts. However, I lived. I helped others live "better" lives.
I took what I had while I had it and enjoyed it.
I went to school, I worked jobs of my dreams.
I helped so much family and friends with food, childcare, money, savings, housing and more.

I never gave to get back. I never not gave because of what I didn't have.

Abundance and gratitude have always overflown.

I think of where I and we are today and all of the drastic little and big changes. I think of how we and I are living dreams right now. Still, and how I have so much more I am still dreaming of.

I think of how others are doing and how I was able to play a part in where they are now. I am thankful for the support I have in and through others, especially in hard times of need that were unforeseen.

I think of how all the puzzle pieces make sense now, or then. even without realizing or knowing.

I think of the memories created and I am just so thankful for the live I have been able to live and the life I live now.

None of it comes without hard times, struggle, pain or challenge.

None of it comes without blessings, gratitude, happiness and abundance.

Right now, we are living some new and old struggles. Right now, things feel hard. I also know right now feels like answered prayers and learning to dream again and more. I know right now, is right now. Right now, is the future memories we will look back on.

Thank you, GOD, thank you heart and soul. For the choices you've made, the people

you've helped, the lives you have changed-
including your own. Thank you, life.
we embrace it all and create what we wish.

2.28.22
Back to work after all the time off. Hello Monday.

I can't believe after all the days "off"
The chalk writing wasn't gone.

This morning, leaving to work was different. It was sunny out already and warm. I got a ride because my husband has the day off so he dropped me off.

To my surprise when I got to work, almost all of the chalk writings were still there even after so many days of time off.

I spruced up the hopscotch and the "dream again". You can definitely see what areas get walked on more than others.

I loved the sun being out this morning and afternoon. It felt so good feeling the warmth on my back.

In the afternoon my whole family came with me. They played at the park up the street and towards the end came to see me and what I do. My oldest daughter said she was inspired. Thank you work, for helping me get up by 6:35 this morning. Thank you work for pushing me to make and drink tea. I did it so I could be warm and not spend money on outside beverages.

So much has taken place because of this work I said yes to.

March 1, 2022
Chalk doesn't seem to last; it goes by real fast.

It's a work day which helps me to wake up at 6:30. Knowing I will have a ride, makes me want to lag. But I am up.
this morning my mom wasn't feeling her best. So, she actually had morning tea with me. I love that I am day two with morning tea.

I do not feel like someone who just had a lot of days off work.
I do not feel like someone who has only worked this job for 8 official days.
Today, I feel pretty drained.
I got rides today, I didn't even bike.
I got sleep last night but I haven't had good sleep in I don't know how long.
At work I feel energized.
Seeing parents and children play hopscotch because I drew it there. Seeing them enjoy the chalk writings. Hearing the conversations. Seeing the smiles, makes me smile. Even in my mask.
"Can I do it today?" one child asks their parent.
In the afternoon I added another hopscotch because it's so much fun for so many. And

although everyone's great at sharing space, why not add another.

"Look there's another one!!!" I hear children scream.

So much excitement.

Today the person who hired me drove by. Asked how I'm liking it. I said I love it. He said "that really warms my heart."

Not sure how long he's been watching or if he's driven by on other days.

But I've always wondered if he would.

Timing seemed perfect.

Today was colder than yesterday.

March is here but it didn't feel like march madness, more like mindfulness.

Today at work, there were several times I crossed adults only. I get many comments like "You don't have to" a man crossing .

"Oh, my goodness, we aren't used to this. Thank you for being here"- an elderly couple.

"For me? really" a young man.

"You make me feel like a child again" a woman, said smiling.

When we have a job, it is our job to do that job.

Nothing wrong with feeling like a kid again, in a good way.

Why do we associate being a kid with being cared for when it comes to safety, walking to school, childhood memories. Was it good or "bad" experiences?

So many thoughts and questions running through my mind.

Yes, you too are worth it.

March 2, 2022
Show up for yourself, as yourself. You never know who is watching and who you will connect with.

My dare and challenge today is to bike to work and without music. What do you see? What do you hear? What do you smell? What are your thoughts? What are you grateful for? I ask these questions while recoding on my bike ride. To my surprise, some people responded.

Someone shared "I see sunlight. I hear the gardeners. I smell coffee. My thoughts are silently praying for my friend's dad. Grateful to be able to live in the moment without worries and have control over my emotions, thoughts and worries." "OOOH, this was good. I liked these questions. I felt the connection, I see what you did here." "It took me awhile to get there but I understand your posts now. I feel like you've been woke. I love when you share your thoughts and journey, it gives me hope to see you succeeding successfully in your goals. Now I understand everything now, I understand why you was always consistent with your peace of mind all these years. Took years of healing and growth but I see you and I am proud of you. You have always had the spirituality and religion in your heart- it took me longer to understand but now I understand why you journal and do affirmations and how you live moment to moment and have peace of mind. To have a happier life. You have paved the way Lena, I am proud of everything you've done and become. It gives me hope for myself." With happy faces and hearts.

Someone messaged me and said they felt like they went on a meditation with me. While another shared "mindfulness at it's best." "It feels great to help people and you do that every day!"

I am so blown away and thankful for how sharing what was going on with me, helped two others reach out to me. It started so much conversation. It gave me conformation that I didn't know mattered. It connected old friends. It helped others reflect. I am just so thankful that social media can reach so many. This afternoon, same path but different views. Its amazing what hours can change. It looks, feels and even has different sounds this time. Deep breaths, water, maybe even time to sit and pause.

I used to walk this path when there was no path. When it was all weeds and dirt and the sight wasn't pretty on either side of the roads. Now, so many years later, I bike and there's bike lanes and walking paths. There's trees and flowers. Beautiful sights and smells.

I have been thinking of decorating the tress. Or making fairy doors. Fairy doors have been a big theme here in Alameda, for several years.

The kids and families make me think of so many things because of their conversations. Like: Masks without choice, Parental advisory, Bullying. living in this new and fear and guidance.

You never know how what you share might impact others.

When others share with you, you could never have predicted what then comes from that.

Inspiration, gratitude, motivation, conversation, reminiscing, reminders and more.

Thank you to any and everyone who's ever liked a post, shared, responded, messaged or anything.

I am so thankful for words, for written words, for embracing moments.

March 3, 2022
Why this job? "Diary of a crossing guard is on my mind."

Riding my bike this morning, through the park that is my mark of being half way there. There is a man spraying the wood chips this morning. Even through my mask the smell is strong. Its unpleasant and probably toxic. But he's just doing his job. I do what I can to speed past but what happens when the toxic lasts, even when you can't smell it or see it happening anymore?

Sneezing in a mask is as gross as the looks you get from sneezing outside of one these days.

I did chalk work. Some kids can read and some ask for help.

"Did you write all of this?" chalk on my pants, so I answer yes.

Questions about the crossing guard before me, "thought you were my sister."

I hear a lady on the phone "we have a new crossing guard now, before- people wouldn't stop for us."

I get scared a child will see me walk into the street and run before it's safe. Scared on foggy days, windy days are hard as well.

I have so many thoughts on my mind, like is there too much chalk stimulation and that thought makes me want to make it disappear.

"I know the answer to this one" a child says.

Questions I hear them ask; I write down to show I hear them.

Bonus level 500 I hear a child say. And I wonder how I can incorporate that into something fun.

The foggy days makes me think of things, questions for myself, questions a child might have. What makes fog? Where are the clouds when it's foggy? A little boy responds after reding and thinking. "Clouds are fog. So, we are in the clouds right now." I love his answer. What if I had that thought this whole time, maybe I would have felt differently about the fog.

Will they always expect this of me? To write with chalk now? What if I run out? What if I can't buy more so often or at all? It goes fast. I borrowed from my kids. What about my kids?

I love being off of my phone, being mindful, being outside, out of my mask, in my mask for short periods of time, breathing intentionally through my nose.

Scared of heatstroke, loving the exercise, excited for the pay, love that I found this job on indeed.

I wonder about the coast guard housing. Living beyond the fence. I watch.

A Puppy laid in the street when crossing. Reminded me of the importance of rest.

"Dream big.... even bigger."

What does it mean to dream? Do you need help? What did you want to be when you grew up? What do you want to be? Who do you want to be? When did you stop dreaming or believing?

Why do we walk our bikes when crossing? Saw someone fall on the scooter, after crossing. Maybe that's one reason why.

I don't write only questions I know answers to. I love answers I hear. Things that make me think too.

Are you carrying others stuff to help them? Does it help you? Do you want to? Do you feel you have to? What can you put down? What can you pick up for you?

Cars rushing around others, not knowing what's around the corner.

Streets I used to walk. Look different now.

People sleeping in cars, bike ride and getting out would show me so much but it's the job that pushes me.

When my shift ended, it started to sprinkle. I did not wish for rain and am not exactly dressed for it but I am thankful it started after my shift. I am thankful for new experiences as I bike ride. Sometimes you get answers or solutions to situations…an answer is an answer- even if not the one you thought of.

March 4, 2022
Finding hearts in the world is something me and my family do, it's like a positive message.

This morning I was feeling tired with a headache and I was feeling in a rush. So, I tried to tell myself to slow down. I asked myself what is the rush telling me is most important? What am I ignoring and setting aside for hustle?

Its wet outside so I have to think fast because my bike was out and I don't want to sit on a wet seat or be in wet clothes doing my job. So, I get a plastic bag and put it on my seat. I feel so smart and creative. Problem solved. Thank you basket of bags, thank you bike, thank you legs. Thankful its Friday.

I made it within 25 minutes which means I have minutes to breathe, drink tea and finish gearing up. I look at the ground, no more chalk. I have a "clean sheet" to create whatever comes next. I found a leaf on the grass; I notice a heart shape in it. Finding hearts in the world is something me and my family do, it's like a positive message.

The wind after my shift ended this afternoon was crazy. It was so loud. Silly of me to see the sun and think I didn't need my beanie and gloves. I am freezing, using my sign as a shield because so much stuff is flying in my eyes. But I am learning.

When you are in a rush. How will you be told to slow down? Fall, spilled drinks, stop light, flat, backtrack.

When the savings and cushion and usual reliable aren't anymore. You have to do different. You gotta do something. I never want to work just for money. I want to enjoy what I do.

Listened to two songs but at one point I didn't even hear the music anymore, just my thoughts.

People I didn't expect to participate, did. What's that say about my perspective?
Age, gender.
Even with the chalk gone, kids participated from memory. They made sounds of sadness "oh no"
Will the income do what I need it to? What might the experience provide?
Not knowing where I would be located but knowing the island. Finding happiness in the possibilities.
"Follow your dreams not your assumptions and fears"

March 7, 2022
The weekend was nice, this morning was even better. Back to morning bike rides. Movement matters, mornings matter, mindfulness matters, making memories I enjoy remembering matters. I can notice the muscle memory in some parts of me now, from biking. I am feeling and noticing the importance of meals and music and seeing all kinds of miracles.
New chalk ideas: I spy. Shadow tracing. Sweet and sour.

March 8, 2022
Build your army you healing queen

They must be talking about lifting masks in schools. Today and yesterday I hear kids talking about it.

"Do you know what happened to the guy that used to be here? He was here for years" someone asks driving by.

What do we make peoples questions mean? Curiosity, concerns.

What do we make their concerns men? Was he working here before or after the pandemic? Am I not doing as good of a job? What did you like about him? Do I have to be him to be loved and accepted? I am curious too. And I didn't know him. What is his name? Is he ok? Why did he stop working?

Does not mean I am a replacement or a fill in. Doesn't mean I have to know or be him.

This afternoon on my way to work, my uncle was sitting at the park. He noticed me going by and decided to bike with me. Someone said to me "He is awesome! Build your army you healing queen." He even sat with me at work. On the way home, we took two separate paths at one point (both saying which way would be the fastest)

March 9, 2022
Same path, new sights, new smells, new experience.

I had created this life in the pandemic and thought I only wanted to work from home.

Then I came across this job and thought this is the perfect job, rainy season is over. Then I remembered, April showers bring may flowers and its only February. I am committed still.

Sometimes we don't pay much attention to what doesn't directly involve us-until it does.

Happy to put on some pants I have had for a while, inspired these days by getting out of leggings.

I made it to work and I had enough time to just sit and chill in the grass, feels good.

March 10, 2022
School is about so much more than education

When I make it to a certain point on my bike ride, I take my time going through the bike path created. I enjoy the sounds and the views. I know when I make it to the end of this path by 7:15- I know I have time to take my time. And if I make it to the end past 7:15, I still have time to make it on time.

As I go passed the college of alameda, I have all these memories and thoughts fill my heart and mind. Like how sometimes you meet that person whose focus is in mechanics but you meet because of the mutual English class. Or maybe you decide to meet because of physical attraction. The point is, you meet and sometimes life lets you become so much more. School is about so much more than education. You are learning about yourself. You are creating experiences that help create your story and life. Sometimes you meet that person who's in the same field as you. And you bond over coursework and new friendships. Sometimes you grow apart and years later one of you becomes an author and the other loses a father to cancer too. Reunited by grief and healing. You can become whatever you believe and not all roads or spaces are everyone's dreams. Trust your path. Degrees don't define who you are. Sometimes people will tell you community college isn't good enough. Or they will celebrate you for being the first in your family with a degree. Or they won't celebrate you. Do you. Be you.

As I work, I notice even when cars aren't coming, I still cross people. Remining them to look both ways. When I remind others, it's also a reminder for myself. I see new faces today.

"Are you the one that has been doing all the chalk work?" I hesitated and then said yes. "I love it all" she says. I almost cry. Not sure why. The appreciation. Doing something right. Fear of doing bad. Happiness.

Two younger siblings stop at the "How are you feeling today?" and there's 3 faces on the ground. Are you happy he asks her?

Another girl says "hey, so and so has the same face this drawing has" I love that my drawing reminded her of a real person and she is making a connection like that. I never would have expected something like that.

"You are out here everyday faithfully; would you like me to bring you tea?" someone says to me. I say no thank you but how thoughtful that is.

The punch buggy who honks, smile and wave. Is an elder man and he always has a smile. He is a car I know that doesn't mind stopping, he never seems to be in a rush and seems to appreciate the job I have.

The Volkswagen filled with all who wave in the morning and afternoon. The many cars of different people in similar vests who wave. I am noticing and observing so much.

I feel like someone important. But am I? I am, because of all I know to be true. My intentions. My work. I am committed until June. How can I keep this longer? Do I want to?

"Thank you for re-doing the hopscotch" a little boy said. Son of mom who asked if I did the chalk work.

Did she ask because most of it has disappeared? She is why I pushed myself to re-draw it and even add more.

March 11, 2022
This morning I took time, to give myself time.

Knowing thoughts come up on my bike rides. Knowing I love time to write and reflect. Happy fri-yay.
What teachings are you bringing to those around you today? Allow moments to teach you.
What are others reflecting back to you, about how you are showing up today?
Think out of the box. Feel your feelings. Safety first.
I create some hopscotch on different sidewalks, that aren't near where I cross guard. I don't have to see engagement take place to know its worth creating space for. I enjoy knowing I am leaving fun the whole way.

March 14, 2022
Grownups feel free to reminisce or dream again.

15 minutes into my morning ride and it was a lot brighter outside than when I started. It took courage to not drive when daylight savings means leaving to work when it's still dark out and a lot colder.
Family funnies.

A guy talked in the street about religious school he went to and how kids helped cross guard. Now girls can do the same job, he says. I enjoy hearing about different people's lives and thoughts.

Early day, made it in 20 minutes. Thighs burning. Sweating.

My boss called and asked if I wanted to be a lead cross guard mentioning supervisor position is available and was wondering if I was interested. As favor to help out he wanted to know about all the minimum dates so I took a little time to help out in that way. It feels good to be able to help. However, the position I signed up for, is the only one I am interested in. I enjoy it. I appreciate the offer but am so not interested. I am happy that I can see my growth in being able to say no thank you and stand up for what I want.

I like to leave questions like "what or who do you want to be when you grow up? (Adults feel free to think back or dream again.)" These questions are not just for children to talk about or parents to just listen. It is a way families can learn about each-other and learn from each-other. It is a way we can all dig deeper and find sparks that maybe we might be ignoring or have been hidden away.

March 15, 2022
Thank you rain. I will be able to create more.

I am grateful this morning for the rain. For erasing what once was and creating new space to create new things. Thank you for the free car wash. For watering the plants. For puddles of fun. For encouraging me to drink warm raspberry energy tea. For encouraging me to wear gloves and take care of my mom. Thankful it's not freezing out or windy- even though it is wet. Thankful its not raining hard. I decided to write on the wet ground. The amount of surprise and shock when adults and kids saw hopscotch on the wet cement. Yep, chalk still works wet.

When you run out of chalk, look around and use what you have. Sometimes I use sticks or leaves or rocks to finish my messages when chalk runs out. I love that I can be creative. I love to show that there is no "one" way to do something. Answers can come in all forms. We can create what we wish, even if it looks different than we imagined.

Today is my daughter's birthday and although I love sun, she loves water and puddles. My dad is present in spirit. You can do all things still, dress for it. Rain and clouds don't mean cold or that there wont be sun. why when it rains, we think about what it's stopping us from doing and what it's taking away and feeling like we need to be extra safe.

Cars are extra crazy today. Let the rain be refreshing.

Two people arguing in the street outside of their cars. One car didn't want to wait, rushes around the other car in front of it not knowing we area in the street. So much is happening that is scary today.

I see one of my family members pass by and share we had other members in a car accident. I have so many thoughts while I'm working. I can't fall apart because I have a job to do. I can't look unstable. I have concerns questions and fears. But I have to be present here.

Why does it rain? I ask questions I hear them have, to show them I hear them. I ask questions I have, in case someone else wonders the same. I ask questions to help conversation and research. I ask questions to spark something in someone.

I help create fun and mindfulness. I help engagement and invite play. I help start conversation and get people involved in intentional movement.

Even if you are showing up just to do your job, you are making impact. Even if its just to get paid or to not be bored. Whatever the reason, you are important.

A guy walking by says "you scratch scratchers?" I say no but my mom does. He gives me one and says "good luck." I think this is such a kind gesture. And on my daughters birthday. So, I play.

His actions were an invitation to play. To do something different. I don't know his intentions but I can make what I want of this situation. And I am just thankful. For nice people.

March 17, 2022
Drained in general

I feel like mornings are earlier with daylight savings. I am leaving the house later these days in hopes of it being brighter out for my ride. Several people are out walking their dogs. I even see individuals sleeping outside. I use my time to take time to pray and hold space for gratitude.

I Knew it without knowing it, todays St Patrick day. I had put on these tall knee-high green socks; I never wear but wanted to today. Thought of the cold. I didn't even check the date this morning. But as I crossed people this morning they said "Happy St Patrick's day!" and that's when I noticed the day but it wasn't until my ride home that I noticed I was wearing green!

Today I made the hopscotch "backwards" today. People still played.

A mom saw me drawing on her way back from dropping off her child and said "it's you !?" it's me I say. She says "thank you, we love them, it's really sweet." Then a child and mom saw, the child says "she made that for me."

Questions pop in my mind like "where does the sun go at night?" and I wonder who knows the answer. I wonder if kids wonder this. Then I think of looking up some facts such as "did you know, spiders usually have 8 eyes" and I noticed the words even inspire me to draw. So, I keep going with each thought. And I google things like "easy kids drawing of a spider." "Do worms have eyes?"

This afternoon my cousin and brother were riding their electric bikes by where I work. And since I was almost off, they waited for me and we all went home together.

Someone stopped by and asked "Do you know what happened to the older man? I ask questions like how long ago did you see him, 3-4 months ago, he was always waiving. I ask his name but the person didn't know. I am thankful for asking questions, for curiosity and for questions.

March 18, 2022
MASKNE IS A REAL THING (acne from a mask)

I love hearing kids ask their parents what certain words say. I love seeing kids sound out words. I love knowing I am promoting ways to ask questions. I love knowing I am supporting children in reading and curiosity.

I was trained to wait at the curb until cars slow down, make eye contact even. So today when a car decided to drive through- it was scary but I was still at the curb. Many parents were upset. I said "that's why I don't leave the curb until it is safe for me and to cross you all." Not long after, a cop parks across the street from me. Eventually I notice him using a speed scanner. Its amazing how much more traffic was mindful and safe with his presence there. Not sure if someone called but he wasn't there long enough.

Another moment a mother said it was ok to cross to her child but I hadn't left the curb and wasn't sure a car was slowing down so I said wait but the child was moving fast in front of her so while holding my sign up I pull him back. That was scary. I explained I need to be sure cars are stopping and we all look both ways. She was so thankful I had helped because that car was so fast and so was her child and she wasn't close enough to "help."

Sometimes we are all assuming about each other. And sometimes those assumptions lead to actions.

I noticed today I have maskne, I have not had any this whole pandemic. Being in this job position is a big change for me, even in this way. I look forward to taking care of myself better. Well, differently.

March 21, 2022
"You are my favorite crossing guard. Because you write things." A child says.

One child says "Know how I'm feeling?" and then jumps on happy face. I ask "is it a happy face?" he says yes. "I'm happy you're happy" I say.

Anytime I ask myself the question if I should let the chalk disappear or not draw anymore, I am reminded why I keep going.

Even when hopscotch disappears or barley shows- they play. Even when two are close together, they still play.

I leave Thank yous and reminders to walk bikes and scooters. Although I say these things all the time when people are crossing, I like to leave friendly reminders.

What do you smell?

"I like your yoda mask". So many have said. It's my daughters, so I thank her for all the compliments.

I want to have a name tag so they can know my name and maybe even share theirs.

It was nice hearing older kids and adults talking about do worms have eyes. Do they? "Never thought about it, they must, I think they have particular cells like eyes."

An older woman was crossing but stopped to read my writings. So, I ask the question she is reading "is there anything that makes you smile?" she said the babies, seeing them happy.

March 22, 2022

The goal was never to give the answer. But to create curiosity to research and experience. To create space for figuring it out and having conversations. Get children experiencing fun with numbers (hopscotch) and movement. Get you thinking and talking. Maybe you'll go teach others or learn from others because of what's written.

I am inspired by a mom and her two boys. The relationship this mom creates with time daily to give space and time for everything from meltdowns to curiosity. Letting others go ahead to give herself peace from feeling pressured. (So I assume)

I notice some who drive by in new or different cars. I notice when faces are missing. I now recognize faces in cars that usually walk.

A young boy stopped at the 6 faces and decides to walk through sad. As his mom was surprised and kind of looked at me maybe in fear of judgement she laughs. We both smile. I smile to let her know I am not judging and I can relate. I smile cause of the intention, honesty, acknowledgement and release I feel like the young boy may have felt.

A High-schooler played hopscotch after reading "anyone can play", I make this assumption based on them walking past , looking down to read and then walking back to play.

A kid looking out the window of a car was reading "what makes you smile?" by the way he was leaning, I feel like he had the intention to read what's written

There was a man on bike and for a long time was unable to cross, so I helped. The cars here can be so focused on their own destination and the traffic can feel like it never ends.

I love this job. But....

What if I just stopped there, that I love this job. No but.

What do you love about this job? What's the struggle?

Today, my husband and oldest son stopped by to visit. It was perfect because I had really been wanting water but didn't have any left. There was some in the car, it was as if I manifested this. It's not like we live on this side, they were driving home from school on my husband's lunch break. And they took that extra 5 minutes to come see me. I love that feeling.

March 23, 2022

Where does your joy come from? Is it attached to how much money you are making? Is it conditional joy based on circumstances?

Still thinking about yesterday. I wonder what it brought for him to name he is sad. Did it spark conversation? Did it get him what he needed? Today his mom decided to use a face to say how she was feeling. Then he took time to think and decides one foot on happy and one on sad.

"Do you write the sidewalk stuff?" a younger boy asks, so I answered honestly.

What has.......

Can you name animals that have horns?

Yesterday a little girl stopped me on my path because she saw my stop sign. So she held out her arm and hand, saying stop. This lasted for several minutes before her mom said "ok, let's let her pass." I thanked her for her help in keeping the path safe.

Today the older man in the punch buggy said good morning, I heard his voice for the first time . He stopped so I could cross people, before I even "asked" him to do so.

March 24, 2022
Every child is born genius.
I am so thankful that even though it's before 7am, it is very bright out.

What are you thankful for?

Someone at home made a hop scotch, thanks to my post.

What is something fun you did today?

I'm a bird that can't fly, what am I?

Yesterday it was me against the wind, today its trash cans.

Today I thought of tic tac toe. I can't exactly leave chalk for people to play so I drew an example and I drew several spaces for people to play. But I used pine cones and leaves as pieces to play.

A guy walking his dog saw me collecting leaves, he sees not far from me chalk on the ground. "are you the one writing the chalk around here? Me and my family always walk through the neighborhood and started noticing"

"We saw something funny earlier, its great someone has a sense of humor" someone said to me. Referring to something I wrote about dancing your sillies out. "The kids are really enjoying it, we all are"

"what's the game today?" "oh, tic tac toe. I hope kids know this game; I know my kids do. Thank you for making us smile"

Have you ever? Riddles, games, I spy, Simon says…. So many games are coming back to mind from my childhood. I am thankful for the memories and reminders.

Are you an empath who wants to save the world? Ever wish you could do more? But you aren't rich enough, don't have enough time, you yourself aren't happy?

How can you create change by just being you? How can you create happiness and spread smiles through masks? How can you make a difference? I found it the way I have many times, with gratitude. Wanting connection. Thinking of children. What do I have? What I have is more than enough. I have chalk, my writing, words, my heart.

March 25, 2022
Its Friday, and payday.

The first thing I didn't do, was check my money. that's a win! That means other things were more important like drinking tea. That means lack and scarcity are shifting and I have more faith in abundance.

I do want to be excited about payday. And I am. But because it means having a home and bills paid. I do miss being able to save or have access and excess.

I hear someone say "who's gonna tell the cross guard? "All 3 boys rush to me. One runs to me "can I tell you a joke to write?" of course "what did the buffalo father say to his son when he dropped him off to school?" BISON. Guy shares he was hit by a car 4 times and almost dies. "Meant to be here"

Kid walking alone yesterday and today who usually walks with his mom, she said she feels safer with me here and knows he will be ok. That is a lot of pressure and a beautiful compliment.

Small boy to girl "you have to walk your scooter. Cause she doesn't like when you don't"

March 28, 2022

I can only share my experiences, information and resources. I can't expect you to have the same experience.

What's in a crossing guards pockets?/vest? What's in my pockets? What do I carry? Have you ever wondered?

March 29, 2022
Want to build connection? It starts with you.

I have gone through 30 pieces of chalk and I just opened this last Monday, its only Tuesday. It costs 6 bucks to buy this pack of chalk that has 50 pieces. But I am creating value.

Yesterday an elder man said "this reminds me of my childhood" stops in the street to talk. I always feel a bit awkward when people stop in the street to talk, I have to ask them to cross fully and sometimes if I have to cross others-then I can't talk. I never want to be rude, so I try to engage and smile and say thank you.

Group of people talking about the bison joke.

Today faces lit up when they saw a new hopscotch.

"Are you the artist creating the sidewalk? Thank you, we love it"

"I am love" little girl said when her mom stops at the how are you feeling section. She jumps on the heart.

"Thank you for writing my joke"

Last Friday I saw the mom I admire, drive by that I never got to tell how she inspires me. Made me emotional. Haven't seen her since and it's Tuesday. I kept wondering if I would ever see her again and if I missed my chance to tell her what I wanted to say.

What are teachers and schools doing? Do you have time to have fun? And take meaningful action?

Get chalk and draw. Let your students inspire, work together or alone. The impact a message has on someone's day is priceless. Thinking of last week, how much chalk and water I went through. Its not about money spent or how fast. Its more like gratitude. Wow, we drank so much water and less wasted bottles. Wow, I helped others find reasons to smile.

March 29, 2022
I cross runners, bikers, homeless, elders, all. It's not just for children or families.

A highschooler walking her dog stops when sees writing. Double looks back to read. Takes out phone to take a picture.

"I am amazing. You can say it. Tell someone why you re amazing"

It's hard for me too. But ill go first.

Need help? Ask someone who knows you.

I don't know you and I know you are amazing.

I hear a mom ask her son why he is amazing. He answered. They share laughs and smiles.

I see a new family walking with babies in strollers and she tells her husband "Look at all of the writings when we walk"

I see one girl hopscotch but she has to start at one before doing it reverse. I had written it "backwards"

I see kids do it literally backwards. I see grown ups do it without kids. I see kids do it on scooters. I see kids take breaks from scooters to do it.

March 31, 2022
"Thank you for all of the chalk work you do, we love it"- a mom walking her daughter says

If you could win an award for anything, what would it be for?

What is your favorite way to move your body?

Today I did a fill in the blank "we don't talk about b_u_o! with a hint, song from a movie.

April 4, 2022
Today I am being photographed for a blog

Today I finally saw her. She was the last one, my alarm had gone off to go home but I didn't rush to leave. I went to tell her how she inspires me. She says her family had a cold for a while. She says she takes her time because one of her sons walk slow and one likes to explore. "Better to make time for exploring than deal with tantrums"

My uncle Kirk saw me leaving this morning and said he likes my earrings. I explained I was going to take pictures for a blog. He said "I don't know what it means but it will benefit you somehow. Someone sees what you re doing. That you don't need to get paid to do good things and have a good heart and spend time." My husband drove me to work to be my photographer…. It's true, someone saw something in me and it inspired them to do a blog about me wearing their clothing. Clothing I already wear, actually the most- ever since I started this job.

I requested time off; I share this because it is a hard thing to do. To know I just started and knowing we are trying to find people to do this work. But I asked for time off because my family and I deserve it. I am approved for May 2 and 3rd off. And I am just so happy that I am supported and that I did this for myself and my family. It is a big step for me and I did it.

April 5, 2022
Sometimes the blinker isn't right. Sometimes people turn a different way.

All march I have been wanting to keep this job. I feel safe to bike ride, I love the impact I am making. I love the community. But now its April and like the families in the coastguard housing, I have to leave. Yep, I recently learned we need to move this summer. It almost seems like it's meant to be, or it can be. That I got this job for a reason and purpose and maybe that's fulfilled. However, I also know and feel life is unpredictable and that we somehow may stay. So, for now I will just be grateful for all options.

Today I met a new family walking. They loved all the chalk. They have big energy. Great vibes.

There's a piece of sidewalk I left blank, to not overcrowd the space- knowing majority of the foot traffic doesn't come that way.

But then I decided to write big in that empty space "what makes you smile?" and a car pulling up saw, the person on the passenger side looked out and read, and was all smiles. I did it for that. The cars that stop at the corner, who just so happen to look out the window. And for the people who can read upside down, because I saw some doing that too.

How did a job I wasn't looking for help me live in my purpose and find my joy. And spark my creativity.

Ever wonder why crossing guards do the job they choose? Ever wonder about their thoughts, fears and life outside of work. I can only speak for me.

I still can't believe I have a Blog and clothing opportunity. That it's really happening. I got the idea offer, accepted. I got the clothing; I took the pictures. And now, we wait. Every step feels so unreal and so rewarding.

April 7, 2022
"it's you, I walk by here just to read what's new. Thank you. For all of your hard work."

Two older men stopped me today and said "it says stop" refering to my stop sign in the front basket on my bike.

This morning I waited until after my morning shift to chalk. Many families that were left, saw. "so, it's the crossing guard, the secret is out"

I hurt my nails and fingers often. Sometimes I take time before or after my shift. A few minutes or 30. Time from my family, money from our house, but it makes me a better mom and teacher and coach and person.

Might be hot later, glad I took this time this morning while it was cooler.

Yesterday I gave a child a piece of chalk. His mom helped me with what to write in the afternoon, when she saw me standing and I said I am thinking of what to write. She said "drink lots of water, its hot"

Today a girl pointed to a face with pigtails and said to her mom "she looks like me" her babies inspired me weeks ago, with a backpack that says follow your dreams.

"I love what you do" people tell me.

If you are new on this path, welcome.

What is your favorite book?

It is thankful Thursday, honestly it exists for me daily but I always remember Thursdays in this way.

April 8, 2022
So many ideas flood my brain when it comes to chalk art.
This or that?
Did you know
Knock knock
Guess the missing word or letter

Trick questions

Can you pat your head and rub your belly at the same time?

Have a great spring break.

If you had 3 wishes.

A woman I never saw before was at the corner turning and said "man these cars drive fast through here. It's a good thing you are here"

"Be safe, stay safe, drink water, hope you have water." Someone says to me. It's a good feeling to know people care.

It's been months of chalk work and hopscotch. Today I did it with shapes. One little girl was so excited.

A boy who walks by often offered me Oreos. They are my favorite but I said no thank you. It was so nice of him though. He is a high-schooler and always so well mannered.

April 9, 2022

What do you call a snail without a shell?

Did you know turtles have more than one shell?

Can you name animals with shells?

If you could have any animal as a pet, what would it be?

April 18, 2022
I was almost in tears of gratitude

What is the best part of your mornings?

A family gave me a bucket of chalk. It was such a surprise. I was almost in tears of gratitude. "Thank you for all you do, we love it." I just had run out. How perfect.

"Lena right?" yes "how was your easter? Hope it was nice"

What's your name anyways? I like that name. he says his name is Oliber.

"Thank you, Mrs. Lena. Have a good day miss Lena"

Kids having tough times, I hear some talking about being bullied and jail

April 19, 2022
Ideas of a Gratitude flower, please leave chalk for others. You may add to it. You can put something even if it repeats.

Scavenger hunt.

Rain washed everything away. Believing yesterday's messages served instead of entertaining thoughts that I wasted my time.

April 20, 2022
"Yesterday we were biking and it was so hard to cross. We are so thankful you are here."
 nice to greet people by name

April 21, 2022
When you can sleep in an extra 15 minutes because you are driving and not biking

How do you give yourself and live in that feeling, on the days "you can't" or "don't have it"
Grateful anyways, thankful still, thankful always.

April 27, 2022
Car in a rush, mom says she is thankful for me

April 28, 2022
"Woah what is that?"
"Wow mom look at that, look at this!"
Lava path
Kid on the phone with someone sharing the knock knock fig joke.
Kids walking alone feeling safe because I am here.
Older guy waits on bike even if I am not there.

April 30, 2022
"Do you still have enough chalk? My kids love what you do. So please tell me when you run low. We all love this"
Guy running said "thank you for being crossing guard" he saw my vest and stop sign when I was at a red light. He shared he did cross guard before for school and saw a massive accident. "We need crossing guards"
Why is sleep important?
 Difference between snow and ice?
Ways to calm down.

How many can you find on your walk?

May 11, 2022
I am so thankful

I am celebrating and thankful for the tears today. Finally, I'm able and not just able but "unable not to." it's been time.

I was cleared to go back to cross guard duties. Almost every family crossed shared words of gratitude and appreciation, sharing how happy they were to see me back and shared how sad they were thinking I may not come back. Kids shared they missed me. Families missed me. I dedicated 45 minutes to chalk work today and I'm so thankful to have felt inspired and energized.

My husbands boss surprised us with breakfast this morning.

My brother-in-law surprised us with lunch. He made one of my favorite dishes!

Surrendered healing got my family dinner tonight through door dash and everyone loved it and everyone shared their gratitude!

Today, we were told that we don't have to move!!!!

I have been crying tears of joy, relief and amazement for hours.

It's just been a day of so much "weight lifted"

And so much clear abundance, manifestations and GODs doings.

May 16, 2022

This morning I was 20 minutes early so that I could do some chalk work. While on my morning shift two groups of kids had jars with something inside. One girl shared while crossing she had eggs that would turn into caterpillars and then butterfly's, she doesn't usually talk when passing by.

Another group of boys, had snails in their container. I was motivated, now I knew what I would do with chalk in the afternoon. Some facts and drawings about snails, butterfly's and caterpillars. I like being able to connect with the kids in this way. To show them I am listening and hear them. In pre-school we would take what interests the kids and build off of it, we would scaffold. Let the children lead.

In the afternoon I put some snail questions and facts, "do snails hear?"

May 17, 2022

This morning I did some chalk work. A woman crossing, not anyone I seen before said "I like your outfit" I said thank you and said "I like your hat." Her hat said "doing my best" she says "you know, I think we all are doing our best. Especially these days I believe it to be true. You are out here working, doing your best. I asked her "what are you doing your best with in life right now?" she said well, like right now, I am going shopping. My husband likes to shop and usually does the shopping but today he is resting his heart. We are so used to working so hard and men feel like they have something to prove in order to "be a man" but as far as today, I'll get him a steak and cook and shop because he deserves a break. I had to cross some families and she continued on her walk. I took out my chalk and wrote "doing my best" with a rainbow like her hat. I wonder if she will see it on her way back.

May 18, 2022
An elder man saw me doing chalk work this morning, he points and says "good job."
Today in the morning I was crossing a family. I noticed a boy on the other side but he still was far away. By the time I made it back across, a truck was blocking the cross walk and my view so I waited but then the boy crossed without me. I felt like I failed him. I thanked him for being safe and encouraged him to wait for me next time. All I can do is suggest and do what I can to keep people safe for the time I am on the clock.
I think about the note I want to leave the families, the last week of school. How I know some of them will move away and how happy they have made my days and life. How thankful I am that they have treated me so kindly.

Today I told a young boy I liked his shirt. He said "I like your stop sign"

5/19/22
A lady who I didn't recognize was driving by and slowed down, rolled her window down and said "Thank you for crossing the kids all the time."

Hop scotch "what numbers are missing?" Kids of all ages stopped to play and answer

I wrote some jokes and I loved watching who laughed and re-told them. And also recognized who just walked over them, I can't let it mean anything about me.

One mom in the morning on her walk back without the kids, saw the busy street and stayed back until it was clear so I didn't feel obligated or rushed. I thanked her for her thoughtfulness.

Girl collecting leaves for days. I wonder what it's for. I think of bringing some to her.

5/20/22
It's pay day. My first with missing days and hours and that reflection. This morning I enjoyed a ride to work, not rushing and enjoyed a chai tea with a morning bread.

A lady walking stopped to red the quotes before crossing. "oh I love that" "I want to take a picture of that one" "that one is my favorite" "I'm coming back to take pictures of all these "I want your job, I love it"

I make the job what it is. Do you really want this job? Positions are available. These are some thoughts that cross my mind, I love comments from others that bring me to reflect. The boys say they found everything on the scavenger hunt. So I ask do I need to make it harder? More challenging? I made it mostly obvious on purpose. Because it feels good to win and have fun. And all ages walk this path. One little girl didn't find the pizza until the end, I had unintentionally put two- they thought I just hid it really well.

Family fun. Competition with siblings. Teamwork with friends.

Thinking of making a challenging bonus round.

Scavenger hunt I had girls in mind because its their favorite. The jokes I had the boys in mind because its their favorite.

5/23/22

This morning I saw a child and family I hadn't seen in a while. I was thinking what if they moved. But I saw them today and was so happy. "Hi Oliber" I feel like I haven't seen you all in forever. I was feeling sick. Well, I am so happy you are feeling better.

Today this afternoon my site supervisor showed up to give me the invite to the crossing guard picnic. I am so excited. I brought up the one thing that has been on my mind, not wanting to be transferred to a different site. He said "I am not moving you, this is your corner, your home" as he was looking at the chalk work art and seeing me interact with the people both crossing and driving by. He mentioned getting us new equipment maybe even beanies or jackets and shirts. He said this school will have summer school but they don't want to pay to have crossing guards so there will be no work this summer.

The group of boys said "the jokes were really good today." And then when I asked if they found all the scavenger hunt items, they said yea. I said even the snake? They said yea, I said not the one from yesterday. I asked if they wanted me to make it harder and they said yeah.

5/24/22

This morning a woman walking, the same woman who loved my chalk work the other day says "hi friend! I still want your job." I mentioned if she really does positions may be open if she looks online. She said thank you so much.

It's a hot morning, no need for double jacket. No time for chalk work this morning even though I woke up early (to make time for show time with my husband.)

This afternoon I was doing chalk work, I got there 30minutes early. A couple walking their dogs saw me, I was writing jokes in spaces of shade and they said "thank you for your messages, we love reading them when we are out walking"

While crossing, a young boy was carrying chalk, I said aww (I thought he was going to do chalk work so I was smiling.) but then mom says "they are for you" they left them by my bike. When they returned after picking up brother from school, I stopped to say thank you and she said "they may not be great to write with but they made us think of you" I told her what I originally thought and she said "aww we should surprise you one day with messages and chalk work" I said you already did surprise me thank you so much this is so thoughtful. This family knows my name and greets me often.

Then another family walking behind them said "great minds think alike, we were thinking of doing the same thing." That same family comes back after picking up kids and ask when my last day is because their children's last day is sooner than this school site.

The same lady who drove by the other day rolled down her window to yell "thank you"

The same boy who said yesterday that he found all the items from the scavenger hunt says "was the second snake under the bush?" I said nope…it's on a red curb and is kind of small and hidden off to the side.

Two days ago I shared how the kids want to try in-person school next year. My fear not being covid but being school shootings, bullying, suicides/ mental health of students and teachers and families.

Last night Iris says "you know the one thing I am scared of...school shootings."

Today, ANOTHER, school shooting. In Texas, but that's still too much for me.

I don't need it to be in Alameda or happen to my kids for it to affect me.

There are children who went to school this morning that aren't going home.

Adults who wont make it home.

Families who sent their children and didn't know it would be their last time ever seeing them.

The fact that my children can access this through their phones, the fact that it is becoming so "normal" is a HUGE PROBLEM.

the fact that they have anxiety to go to school because they don't want to die from something like this is a HUGE PROBLEM

My kids are scared to go to in-person school and are rethinking their decision

Today there was a school shooting in Texas

It has been so heavy on my heart.

As I went to work this afternoon, to cross guard for families.

I thought of those children who were shot today. who were hurt. who were killed.

Knowing their faces and their stories will soon come to be.

The pain! so much pain! AGAIN!!!!!
when does it end?
when are our children safe?
when are we safe?
when will we pay more attention to those who are showing us signs that we decide not to pay attention to, until it's too late.
The news is so hard to watch. I don't even watch the news.
but you can't even get on social media without seeing what's happening today.
and they deserve to be seen. to be known, to be remembered.
to feel the pain.
but man, it's hard

5/25/22

I'm up at 4am, I went to bed knowing some families couldn't go to bed because of broken or frantic hearts. For your child to be missing in such a time, to have to identify bodies through dna, to know your child or loved one is gone.....
To know my kids are home safe
But never know how long they will be safe from situations such as what took place
My heart hurts
It needs to hurt
Because we all need to be outraged, hurt and fight for change
Fight for better

They deserved it. They deserve it. We deserve it. Our future deserve it.

Tough morning cross guarding. Keeping my feelings in check.
Keeping the tears from releasing.
Saying Good morning to all the beautiful people, when it hurt me to say good morning and yet brought so much gratitude.
Thinking of the shooting in Texas yesterday, it's like I can't not think about it. About them. Their faces.
Someone walked them to school yesterday…said see you later or goodbye or good morning.
That moment in time must have been terrifying and painful.
I hope the day was filled with smiles. But days can also be hard. Who knows what days each person was having, even before that horrible situation took place.
We know some celebrated ceremonies and awards just hours before.
Some dressed up and many looked forward to summer just days or even moments away.
I can't stop the thoughts.
As I woke up this morning to get my family ready for my son's 5th grade graduation, it is very conflicting feelings of fear and gratitude, sadness and excitement.
Yes, all these feelings are present for me.

But it's been a tough morning. To process and move with life, as others' lives have stopped, turned upside down and changed.
For some it's a good morning.
I am thankful to be here.
I am grieving for those lost and hurting.
If you need today to be "normal", it's ok.
If you are numb to this by now
If it's too overwhelming
If it's a good day for you, today….
—— it's ok
Feel your feelings
Be with your journey
Live your life
It's ok to be human
Holding it all
The anger, grief, confusion, rage, gratitude, anxiety, pain, fear, —- all of it
—- today is tough
And as a collective we have to create change

people are living with thoughts and regret and guilt that shouldn't be theirs. but, we are human.
this could not have been predicted.
"I should have said good-morning to you"
"I shouldn't have worked on your birthday"
"You asked me to stay home and I didn't let you"
"why didn't I take you home after the ceremony"

"I should have rushed in the school to save you when the police weren't doing it"
"I never bought you that phone"
"I didn't see the signs"
"I wish we talked more"
....
the list goes on. it is heartbreaking.
we need to be here for each other.
we need to be aware our words and actions hold so much power.
our intentions and attention have value.
feel your grief.
grieve.
there is no time frame or no "way" to do this.
just allow yourself what you need.

5/26/22
Hello 4am, we meet again.
I had this thought, the night of the day the texas shooting took place. And, I have it again this morning.
what if , that the next day- the whole world shut down? like we did for the pandemic.
what if all "parents" decided not to send their kids to school the next day.
what if teachers decided not to show up?
what if the world stopped, to put in thought and actions- right after this?
i know that, that wouldn't be ideal for everyone. everyone is not feeling this the same way. some people don't feel affected.

some people aren't. some are ignoring all the things.

you are entitled and more than allowed, to feel how you feel. whatever it is that you are feeling.

but, if we did something as a collective, how powerful would that be?

would that give people the space to feel their feelings.

parents were scared but still dropping their kids off the next day, because they had to. they had to go to work. their kids are expected to show up. everyone has to make money.

or maybe they just want consistency for their kids and to shelter their kids and to keep a smiling face.

whatever the reason , we should be there for each other.

cause this is another part thats playing into mental health, peoples mental health, people not feeling protected. people not feeling deserving, to take the time that they need- to go through something!

there's not enough help for people out there. people aren't feeling safe.

your thoughts become your actions.

now, what about the people who dies? what about the people hurting?

what about the people who are angry because police decided to only go in for their own children or the fact that they waited so long to go in and help!

what about all those people? what about everyone affected?

what about them?

who will they turn into? what kind of support will they have?

what about our children?

what about our school safety? that shouldn't even be an issue!

what are we going to do?

why are we still pushing through with hustle? and all of these things to go on about daily life like this is normal. it should not be normal!

our kids deserve better. we deserve better! we can do better.

we learned through the pandemic that there is time. there is time to take time. that people can wait. that things can change. that there is enough money to make changes and to help. we have learned so much.

and yet, its like we are falling right back into...whats always been .

what if we took more than a moment of silence?

what if we took a day. or days. or a week. or weeks. or months. or a pandemic time.

what would we accomplish then?

what could we accomplish then!

what change could we create?

yes, that doesn't work for everyone and we need also may need to be there for people in the struggle, with the people struggling. or with the people who would struggle because of such change.

but, i also know...if you don't do different, you don't get different!

we have to do something different.

just like the street I am working on where speeding is an issue and i am a crossing guard. i almost get hit, too often and people are not the nicest. the city is trying to create change, thinking of putting in bike lanes on the side and making it more beautiful and what not. and, of course my first thought is "but what is that going to do about the speeding?" then my next thoughts are "but any change for the better is good change. i am thankful they are wanting and willing to make changes. it will give space for bikers and walkers to feel a little more safe and be a little more safe and protected." and we can still work on the speeding street, we will still have to. speed bumps, lights, more than signs because the signs aren't working, me as a crossing guard isn't always working. i say all this to say its the same thing.

ok, our schools shouldn't look like jails. with metal detectors and security, we shouldn't need those things to make sure we are safe. but, it could be one way. changing gun laws don't necessarily mean the people who want the guns wont get the guns and do what they are going to do, but- maybe it will. maybe it would have changed the one that happened recently.

we don't know. and the point is, we have to try. because it could make a difference. and, doesn't that matter?

what if we all just took the time we needed, for selfcare and self love?

gave ourselves permission to just have a day with our children and families. not needing the weekend or a holiday to allow for that. what if we gave ourselves permission to grieve? or permission to take meaningful action, for change?

what if, we do things as a collective. it doesn't have to be done the same way or affect someone the same way to still give ourself permission and time, to take the time- to take care of ourselves for whatever that means.

what if, what if we did.

what if we took the time to have to feel our feelings? to look at the situations, to see the faces, to let it matter to us and affect us.

what if,

would something change?

A mother and two sons passed me this afternoon, and handed me a bag with 3 cookies. This is the same family that gave me chalk days ago but the child who is usually in school wasn't there. He wanted to be a part of something since he missed out on chalk, so they made and gave me cookies. Reminded me of my favorite funfetti cake.

Today I stopped a boy bike riding to tell him that I have been noticing someone saying things to him and I wasn't sure if that's a friend or if they are joking /playing and he quickly said she isn't joking. I told him bullying is never ok and that I hope he has people he can talk to, that I can see he is a good kid and I just want to make sure he is ok. He said he can talk to his mom and dad and thanked me for checking in with him.

Besides looking at tomorrow as a day of "not making money, not having cross guard shifts" I still have another job and other ways to make income thanks to surrendered healing and authorship.

I will look at tomorrow and Monday as a day to be more present with my children and family. Time to rest. Time to enjoy all that I enjoy. Time to do the things "I never seem to have time to do."

I will look at those two days as extra time for self-love and self-care.

the income will handle itself.

thank you GOD for time, for space, for mindset shifts and perspective.

5/27/22

No work day

The news is really hurting these days.

I want a break
And I want to learn from it all
I want to better protect and serve
Anything at anytime can happen to any of us
Whew, my heart

5/30/22
Monday, no work day. Morning walk.
I say to my husband how I noticed soccer has really brought life back into him.
He says "like I didn't have life before?"
I say of course but this is so very different and noticeable. Pure happiness
It's like me with writing, you with soccer
He says "yea, I'm a poet with the ball"

Yesterday I started typing up stargell and mosley, diary of a crossing guard. Decided I want it complete by August.

5/31/22
Back to work. Hello Tuesday. Got there 15 minutes early to do chalk work. One mom asks if I will be cross guarding for the summer school. Another says "I hope you had a good weekend."
whew, this summer I am on a quest to visit Burney Falls, Write my next book "diary of a crossing guard" , get back to practicing yoga, spending intentional time with my family and preparing for our household to join in-person school next year.

I want to travel, receive taxes, and work on my dreams/goals. I want to have fun, rest and get stuff done

6/1/22
Almost hit by a car. She wouldn't stop moving forward even with eye contact and slowing down.
Heard one little girl say with a leaf she picked up, I am going to make a barbie dress.
 I ran out of chalk.

This car and I made eye contact, I was in the middle of the street, they slowed down (a family at the corner ready to cross) and, the car never stops! Continues going! Thank goodness that family never left the curb and were looking out for me🙏
This street has moments of calm but so many moments of crazy and scary situations.
I know I can't assume much but what I assume is this person felt like the pedestrians werent crossing fast enough and decided to keep on going , even with me in the street- less than an inch away from their car!
I wish I had time to get a license plate but doing this work is a very busy job and I have no time to be cross guard and photographer/police officer.

I have been getting up even earlier than my 6:30 morning goal time. I have been getting up at 6, and today was one of those successful days. I biked my morning shift, but then my mom came over and decided to drive with me to my afternoon shift. She even sat out on the grass while I worked. she was upset about my recent incident with this street.

we paid our rent today. although it is still challenging by at least $500, and thats with family helping us with some groceries. we borrowed and made it. knowing payday is this friday and I now have an extra income but also knowing one income will pause for summer break.

everything is so bittersweet.

Last month my favorite democracy jeans ripped on the inner thighs...I continued to wear them...and today, I let go and said goodbye.

This was hard for me. I think of the money spent, what it took for me to spend.

But , I am so proud of me. For purchasing those and that I own several democracy jeans.

I am proud I let go, letting go is hard for me.

I am thankful for all of the days that these jeans have served me. For the bike rides, date nights, work days, walks---the comfort they brought and the way they made me feel. I had to try democracy jeans for myself in order to be able to share my truth about them.

They are my "go to" jeans since having my 3rd child.

I spent much of the pandemic time in leggings and sweats but these have been my "dress up" item.

letting go, is a process.

deciding on decisions, is a process.

and I am so happy with the choices I have made.

6/2/22

So much has surprised me about this job. From the very first day I was so surprised about how much I loved it. To this date, that feeling and truth has only grown. I've been able to build meaningful relationships with children and families and give input to the city about how to help improve the area and roads.

6/3/22

Friday. I love paying off credit cards on pay day. Time to be even more intentional when spending.

Ever wonder what is on a crossing guards mind?

Fears on the job?

What he/she might be carrying in her/his pockets?

Why they wear certain clothing?

Why we ask you walk your bike/scooter when crossing?

Have you ever wondered how to have more fun at work?

How to connect with others when you have on a mask or no time to socialize when crossing the street?

Ever wonder how to create impact beyond the job description?

Can you love the money you make? By loving what you do.

Even on the hard days. The foggy days, rainy days, cold days, hot days. The days where you don't feel like getting up and want to snooze the alarm. The holidays of not being paid. The summer of no work.

Have you ever stopped to thank your crossing guard? Share your name? Say hi?

.....well, this summer I'll be working on my next book "diary of a crossing guard"

What journey are you on? Do you have a destination in mind?

6/6/22

Monday. Extra early day. Biked both shifts. Met up at sand castle picnic area beach to meet cross guards and eat food and hang out. I got a shist and won beach towels from a raffle. My mom, athnea and leo joined. I got a pin to put on my vest that says "you are truly appreciated" and was told I got that as a rookie of the year award.

Haven't had a morning ride in awhile.

So many mixed thoughts.

I have to get home for a 9am appointment

(If I drive I'd for sure be I. Time and with time to settle in)

morning ride means morning movement, morning exercise.

fresh air, drinking water, time with me and my thoughts.

kids are safe with hubby.we don't need a sitter. So happy our schedules allow for this teamwork

is this a preview of life to come? The next school year when Leo and iris are in person school.

Things will be far more hectic with kids needing to get ready and drop offs and what not.

I am reminded why I love school from online. My oldest daughter can get work done from anywhere. Currently she's sleeping over at families where she has math support and acces and flexibility.

will in person learning mean I am giving up the life I love, we love, that we have created? Worked hard to create ?

(Knowing nothing is permanent and also my fear/anxiety is screaming loud when it comes to issues like mental health, suicide, bullying, school shootings,time management and peer pressure)

I don't want to live in or live by fear. I want to partner with it and lean into faith. Lean into human connection, support, building independence and being open minded

I keep trying to "figure out" next school year.
Wanting to have a plan. but all I have is ideas that feel chaotic because all of them mean change from this life I enjoy from a life I have been avoiding.

(Kind of feels like back to the grind: figuring out work, sitters, school, schedules, fears) does it have to be that way? Even if we choose into change.

We have choices.

I am biking to work and see a familiar face. We share words.

A simple how are you or how's it going, can lead to so much. Within 5 minutes she said this amazing opportunity she has and in the same breathe says "but I really want to start my pet business but I don't know"

I say "we'll it sounds like you know"

And she says "wow I do huh!" In amazement and realization.

literally a two way street of realization and exhale for us both. Of course with that comes fear and everything else. But, all you need is the next baby step.

That's all it took. (Of course it takes foing but it starts with our thoughts)

And this, this is why I need to be a coach.

I literally have someone asking for another session and to pay me!

GOD is answering all these prayers and wishes.
I just need to say yes and follow through

6/7/22
Tuesday. Today is the second time someone told me I should make a separate ig account for my cross guard journey. I think my title would be cross guard chronicles.

oh my goodness, the gifts I got from families this morning truly took me by surprise and touched my soul. So thankful.
The children were so excited to give them to me. As they were crossing I could here "did you give them to here...I want to" They waited until I made it back to the sidewalk and I was handed so much at once. "do you like purple, i made you this one"
"this one is from me, i even put your name"
I had to cross another family and even after that I feel like I didn't get to really show them how thankful I was.
But, it wasn't until I got home and really was able to look and take my time. The notes! the cards, the thoughtfulness. I was moved to tears.
minutes later I was handed another small bag and was told cookies were inside. However, I didn't expect o see what I saw when I got home! They had a note written on the cookies for me!!!!

"tomorrow is the last day we will see you because we are moving next week" sad face another mom gives me a loaf of sourdough bread. she says they are moving in two days!!!

I don't have favorites but I feel like all my favorites are leaving.

and then another mom , walking with her two sons and husband asks "will you be here next school year" and I say yes. and I am so excited to hear someone is staying.

This afternoon I make s thank you note on the sidewalk with chalk. Because it's hard to have conversations while "on" the job.

One of the little girls crossing this afternoon says "I hope you like our gifts"

I said I did so much I hope you see the note I left you all

My heart is so filled. I'm sad, thankful, inspired, motivated and filled with happiness

6/8/22
Last day of school
My mom says this morning "wow I didn't know cross guards get gifts"

I said me either

Unexpected but so grateful

Do you have a crossing guard you are thankful for? I encourage you and invite you to give a gift if you feel moved but more than anything, share your words.

Do you wish your neighborhood had a crossing guard?

Do you recognize the role of your community crossing guards?

Just like teacher appreciation, I think all titles and roles and people deserve to know they matter beyond a paycheck.

Let someone know why you appreciate them including yourself

Whew!!!who knew today would be so emotional!!!!. I look forward to next school year being their crossing guard

Today, I deleted my alarm for this work until august.

Asked my questions about leftover sick time(learned it rolls over) and unemployment. I wonder if I will be able to figure out unemployment benefits, that was something that interested me when I learned about accepting this job.

We shall see

During the summer, I learned we don't have to move. I will indeed be back

Why do you do the work you do? Why did you choose your job?

_____

_____

_____

_____

_____

_____

_____

_____

_____

_____

What would it look like to be the best version of yourself?

_____

_____

_____

_____

_____

_____

_____

_____

_____

What are you worth an hour? Why is your time and talent worth that price?

_____

_____

_____

_____

_____

_____

_____

_____

_____

_____

How do you place value on yourself?

_____

_____

_____

_____

_____

_____

_____

_____

_____

_____

What kind of job description is ideal for you?

_____

_____

_____

_____

_____

_____

_____

_____

_____

_____

How can you expand your world today?

_____

_____

_____

_____

_____

_____

_____

_____

_____

_____

In what ways are you making a difference in the world?

_____

_____

_____

_____

_____

_____

_____

_____

_____

_____

Have you ever underestimated yourself? What did that teach you?

_____

_____

_____

_____

_____

_____

_____

_____

_____

_____

How do you hold space? What are qualities you bring to places you show up?

_____

_____

_____

_____

_____

_____

_____

_____

_____

_____

What did your yesterday teach you?

_____

_____

_____

_____

_____

_____

_____

_____

_____

_____

How did it shape you, today?

_____

_____

_____

_____

_____

_____

_____

_____

_____

_____

Why does money matter, what does it bring to your life?

_____

_____

_____

_____

_____

_____

_____

_____

_____

_____

What would it look like to live a life you love?

_____

_____

_____

_____

_____

_____

_____

_____

_____

I invite you to think of a chore you do that isn't so "fun" How many of your favorite songs can help you get it done? (share your experience)

_____

_____

_____

_____

_____

_____

_____

_____

_____

_____

Time to celebrate. Let's celebrate time. (What did time give you today?)

_____

_____

_____

_____

_____

_____

_____

_____

_____

_____

What did you give yourself time for?

_____

_____

_____

_____

_____

_____

_____

_____

_____

_____

Love is...............

_____

_____

_____

_____

_____

_____

_____

_____

_____

_____

_____

About the Author

Diary of A Crossing Guard, Stargell and Mosley is Author Carolina's 5th self-published book (4th for distribution.) Carolina, also known as Lena has taken a break from being a pre-school teacher and embraced inner healing. Part of that healing path has been learning to dream again and say yes to those dreams, such as becoming an author. She loves being a wife, mother, friend, daughter, teacher, coach, sister and author. Right now she is enjoying living in the moments and can't wait to get her first and future children books created.

A note to my readers

I hope if you take anything away that you get curious, ask questions and invite play. Whoever you are, however you ended up on any page of this book- I thank you and celebrate you.

Diary Of A Crossing Guard

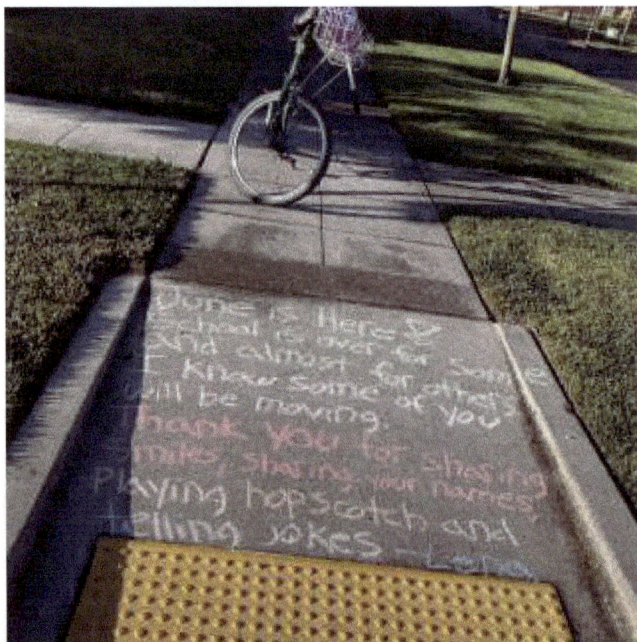

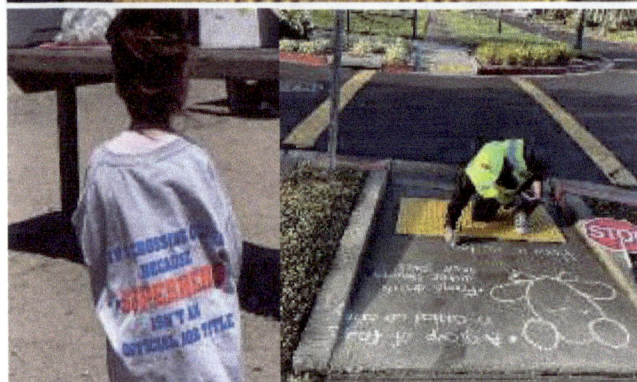

Moving means you
get to see more of
the world. And more
of the world gets to
know you. Enjoy your
new adventures

Lena Ayala-Velasquez

My book goal and
challenge for myself
this year is to write a
"tiny" book. Today I
decided it will be "Diary
of a crossing guard"

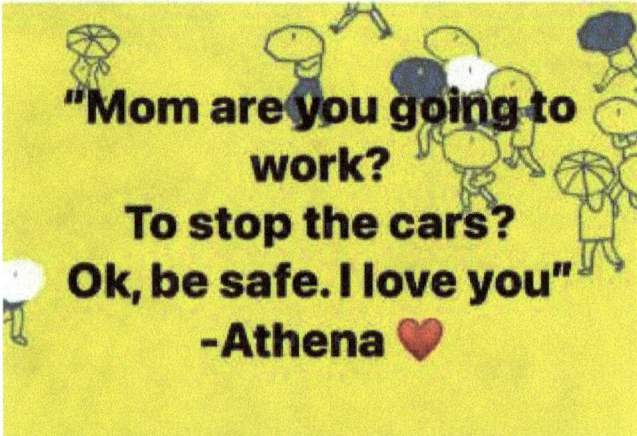

Lena Ayala-Velasquez
2h ·

"Mom are you going to work?
To stop the cars?
Ok, be safe. I love you"
-Athena ❤️

Part 2 will be out in 2023, until next time. Do the work that lights you up.

www.ingramcontent.com/pod-product-compliance
Lightning Source LLC
Chambersburg PA
CBHW070123030426
42335CB00016B/2249